T0067515

Inspirational Activity Book

Written By
Sarah and Andrew Honaker

Illustrations by
Janet Hayden & Elizabeth Middendorf

authorHOUSE®

AuthorHouse™
1663 Liberty Drive
Bloomington, IN 47403
www.authorhouse.com
Phone: 1-800-839-8640

© 2014 Sarah and Andrew Honaker. All rights reserved.

No part of this book may be reproduced, stored in a retrieval system, or transmitted
by any means without the written permission of the author.

Published by AuthorHouse 10/08/2014

ISBN: 978-1-4969-4345-3 (sc)
ISBN: 978-1-4969-4344-6 (e)

Any people depicted in stock imagery provided by Thinkstock are models,
and such images are being used for illustrative purposes only.
Certain stock imagery © Thinkstock.

This book is printed on acid-free paper.

Because of the dynamic nature of the Internet, any web addresses or links contained in this book may have changed
since publication and may no longer be valid. The views expressed in this work are solely those of the author and do
not necessarily reflect the views of the publisher, and the publisher hereby disclaims any responsibility for them.

KJV
Scripture quotations marked KJV are from the Holy Bible, King James Version (Authorized Version). First published
in 1611. Quoted from the KJV Classic Reference Bible, Copyright © 1983 by The Zondervan Corporation.

Hello Friend,

My name is Andrew. My mommy and I have started this inspirational activity book for you. It contains powerful quotes that my mommy and I read which gives us strength when we need it.

I would like you to read the quotes and think about people who display those qualities or a time when you have felt that way. You may add the picture of the person you are thinking of, write your thoughts, draw and color in the frame boxes provided. My mommy has helped me add in some of our thoughts and stories to get you started.

This is your book and I would like you to add quotes you like. This is just a start and I know with your thoughts you will add many.

Hugs,
Andrew & Mommy

1

I've learned that people will forget what you said. People will forget what you did, but people will never forget how you made them feel.

- Maya Angelo

What are your thoughts?

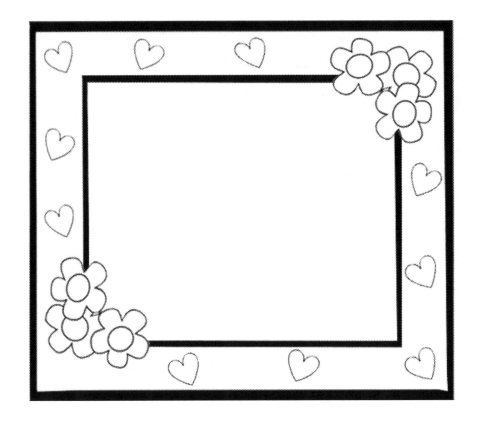

What does it means to me?

When I was playing with my best friend at his party he did something to me which wasn't nice, but then said he was sorry. I don't remember what he did but I did feel good that he said he was sorry. Feelings matter.

Faith in God includes faith in his timing.
                                    -Neal A. Maxwell

What are your thoughts?

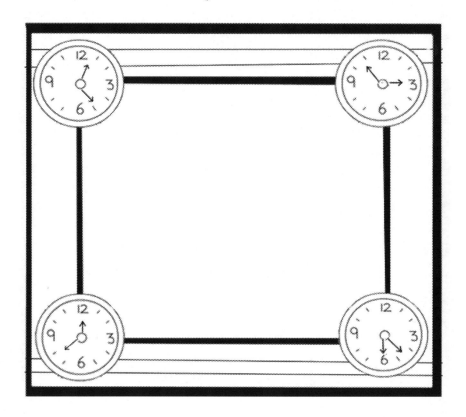

What does it mean to me?
I am starting to learn to read and sometimes I get really frustrated when I don't know the words. I just want to be able to read and my mommy tells me I need to be patient and practice. I know in time I will be able to read. Be patient.

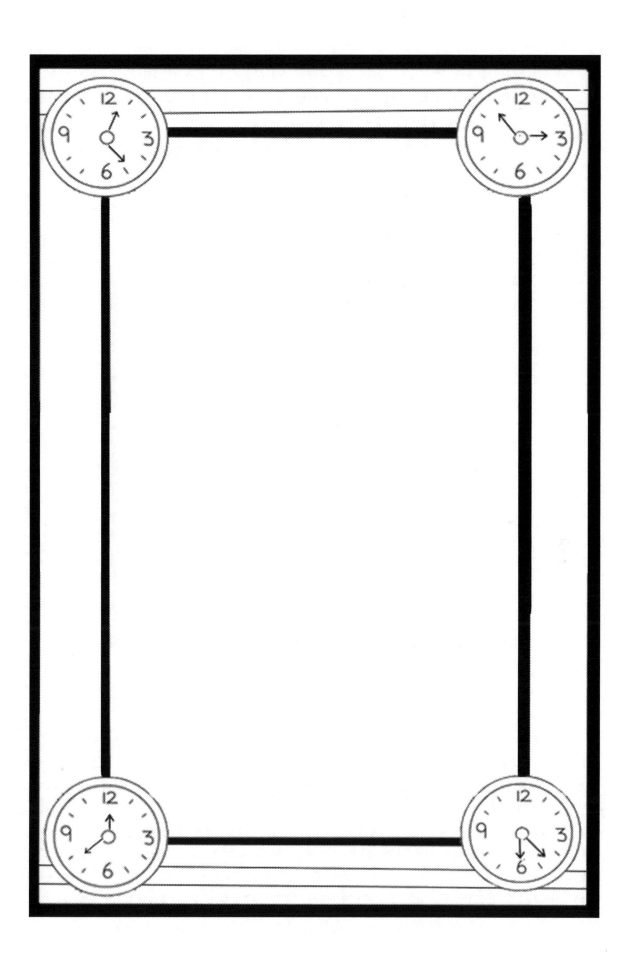

Everybody is a genius. But if you judge a fish by its ability to climb a tree it will live its whole life believing that it is stupid.

-Albert Einstein

What are your thoughts?

What does this mean to me?
I think about my mommy on this one. She is a pretty good runner. We ran at the park today together. My dad said she isn't a good cook. My mommy said she would have to agree she burns things. So if you were to judge my mommy on her cooking skills alone she wouldn't be good and she wouldn't think good of herself. Play on your strengths not your weaknesses.

Two roads diverged in a wood, and I took the one less traveled by and that has made all the difference.

-Robert Frost

What are your thoughts?

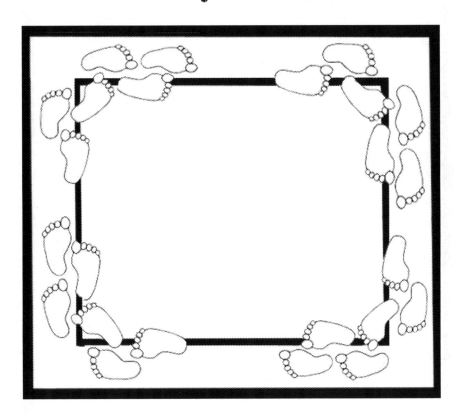

What does this mean to me?
My grandparents' good friend Chuck always did what he believed was right, not just what the crowd did. Even though people disagreed with him he still did what he thought was right. Many times he was right and was a very successful businessman. Do what you believe is right. Don't always follow the crowd.

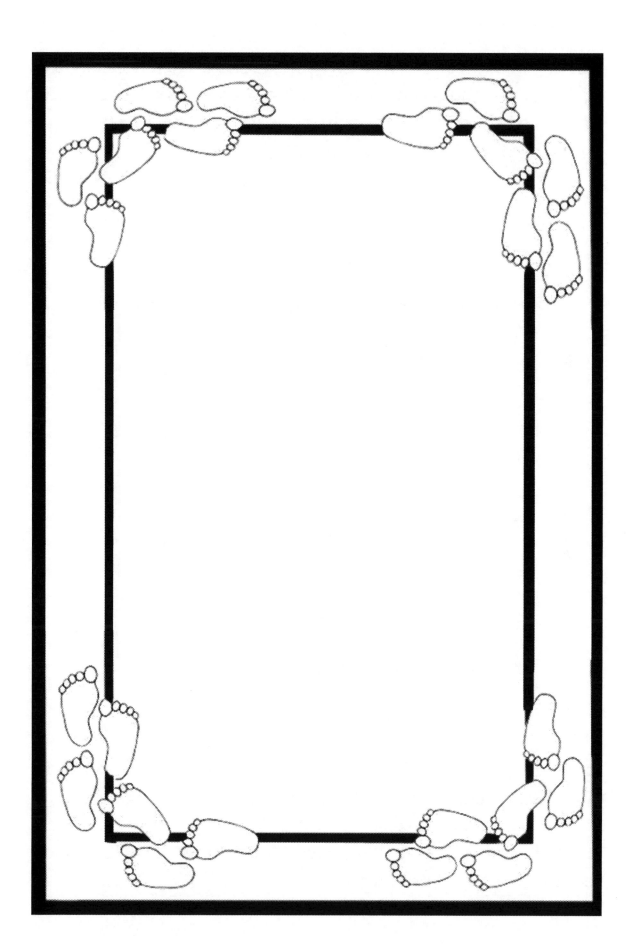

Never apologize for being sensitive or emotional. It's a sign that you have a big heart and that you aren't afraid to let others see it. Showing your emotions is a sign of strength.

-Bridget Nicole

What are your thoughts?

What does this mean to me?
Sometimes I get my feelings hurt at school when a friend doesn't want to play with me. I sometimes act out and cry. I don't mean to cry it just comes out because I am sad. It is okay to show your feelings.

God has a reason for allowing things to happen. We may never understand his wisdom but we simply have to trust his will.

-Psalm 37:5

What are your thoughts?

What does this mean to me?
I think about my Nanny on this one. She has had two husbands pass away. Not for sure why they were chosen to go. I am proud of my Nanny that she keeps going and moves on even though I know her heart hurts when she thinks of them. Keep faith in God's plan.

Maybe Christmas doesn't come from a store.
Maybe Christmas perhaps means a little bit more.
-The Grinch

What are your thoughts?

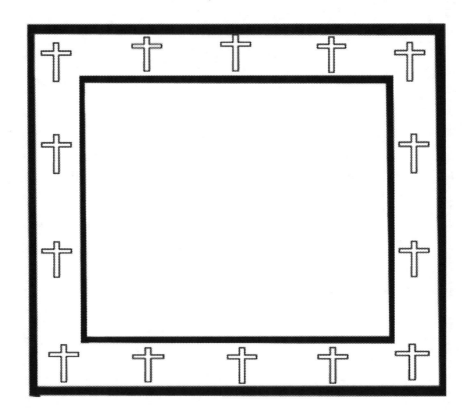

What does this means to me?
I know that Christmas is about Jesus being born and that we should celebrate his birthday and spend time with family and friends. We should show our loved ones how much we care about them. Christmas is God's gift to us, he gave us his son Jesus.

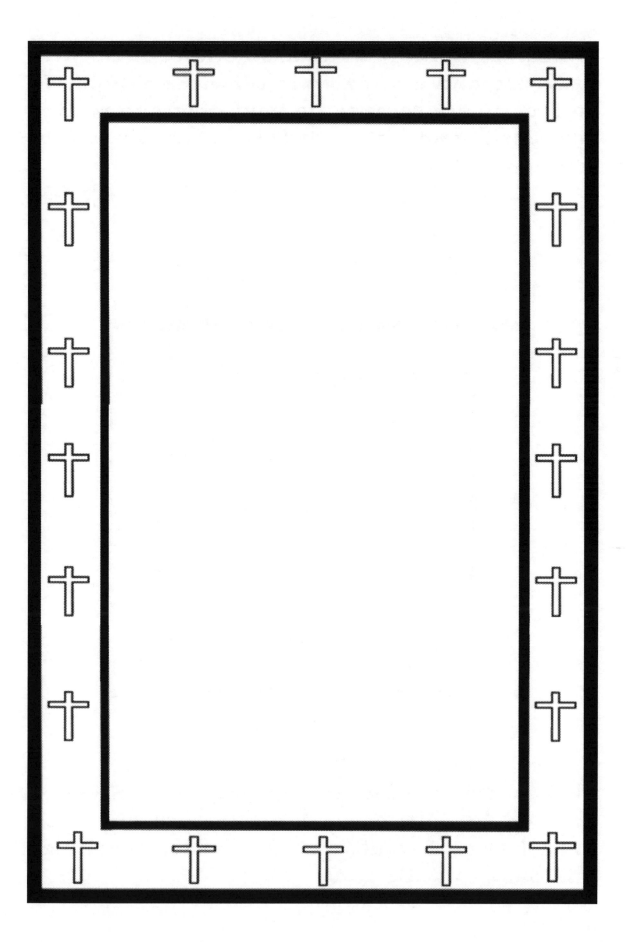

Sometimes walking away has nothing to do with weakness, and everything to do with strength. We walk away not because we want others to realize our worth and value, but because we finally realize our own.

-Robert Tew

What are your thoughts?

What does this means to me?
When a boy on the playground pushed me, I decided to walk away. I didn't push him back since I knew I would get in trouble. Sometimes it is okay to walk away.

You can do anything but not everything.

-David Allen

What are your thoughts?

What does this mean to me?

My Ganpa is very good at many things. He is a good businessman, family man and is active in his church. He always says to focus on the things that matter in life: your family, church, friends, health and hobbies. Focus on things that matter in life and what you enjoy. Don't spread yourself to thin on things that don't matter in your life.

1 2 3 4 5

1 2 3 4 5

I've seen miracles just happen silent prayers get answered broken hearts become brand new that's what faith can do.

-Kutless

What are your thoughts?

What does this mean to me?
Recently my Gamma had not been feeling well and we were so worried that she could be really sick with a bad illness. She had to have tests run and my mommy was very sad. We prayed to God that she didn't have the really bad illness and Ganpa did too. Ganpa even lit candles at the church. Thanks to God he answered our prayers. Prayers work.

A good laugh and a long sleep are the two best cures for anything.

-Irish proverb

What are your thoughts?

What does this mean to me?
I think about my Great Grandad he is very silly with me and always makes me laugh. I know every time I see him he makes me smile and cheers me up with his funny noises. Laughter is a great medicine.
I also sometimes don't go to bed on time when I should. When I do go to bed on time I always feel better and more rested in the morning. A good night sleep helps.

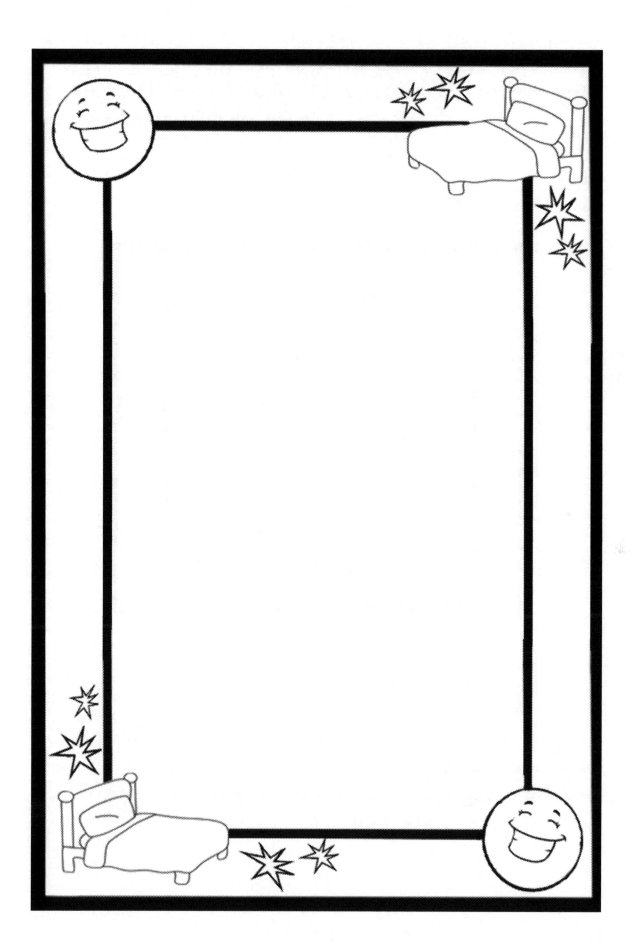

What lies behind us and what lies before us are tiny matters compared to what lies within us.
-Ralph Waldo Emerson

What are your thoughts?

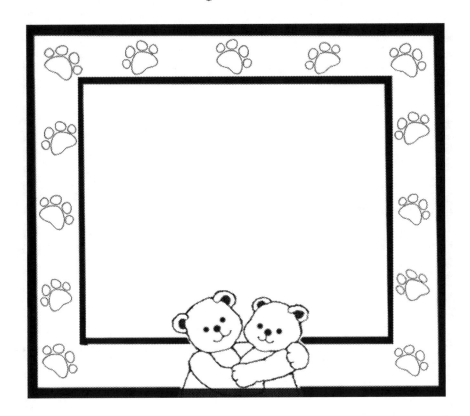

What does this mean to me?
My mommy helped me with this one. I guess it doesn't matter as much as what is coming or what has happened. It matters how kind we are and how big our hearts are to help and care for others. Have a big heart and care for others.

Unless someone like you cares a whole awful lot, nothing is going to bet better. It's not.
                                        -The Lorax

What are your thoughts?

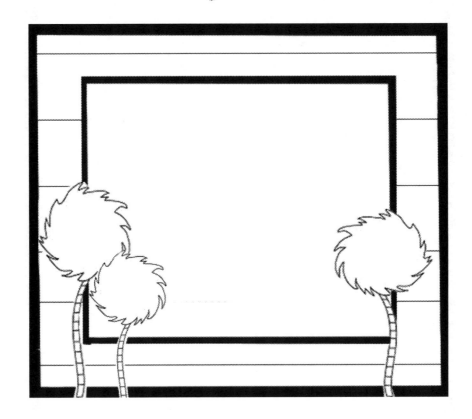

What does this mean to me?
I really care about writing this book with my mommy. We want this to help other boys and girls build confidence and learn that sharing our feelings is a good thing. Effort counts.

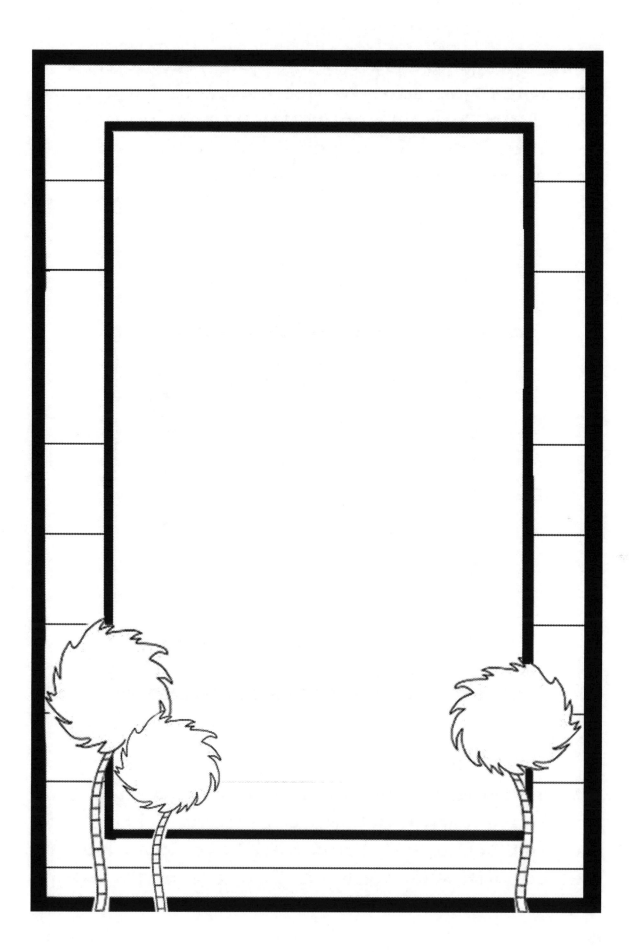

When things are bad when you feel sour and blue..when you start to get mad..you should do what I do..Just tell yourself, Duckie, you really are quite lucky! Some people are much more..oh ever so much more unlucky than you!

-Dr. Suess

What are your thoughts?

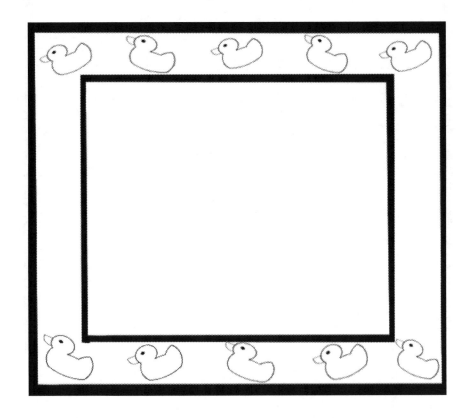

What does this mean to me?
I know there are really sick kids and kids that don't have very much food or love. I hope that they get better, get food and have love. We are blessed with what we have. Count your blessings.

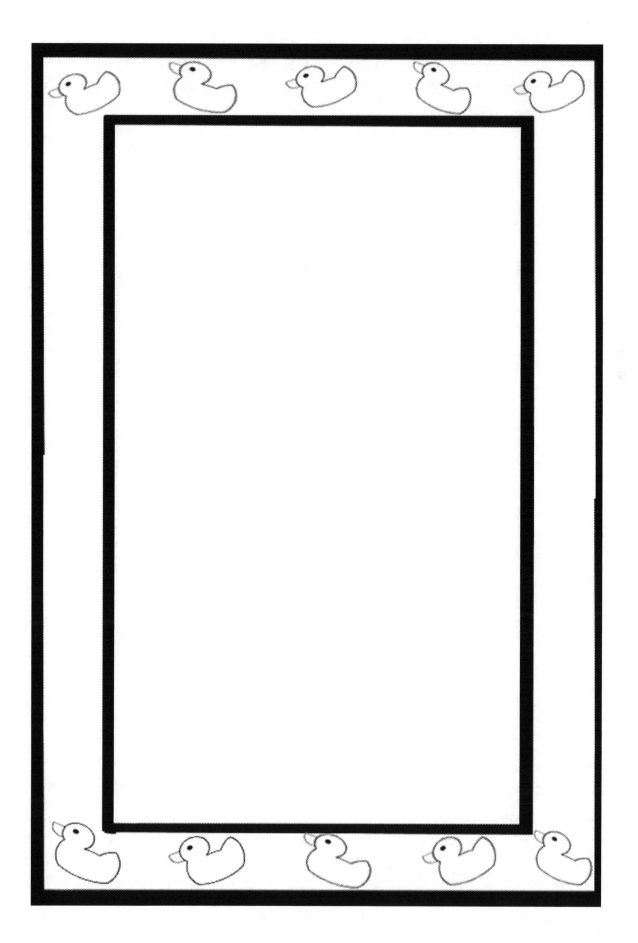

I don't believe you have to be better than everybody else. I believe that you have to be better than you ever thought you could be.

-Ken Venturi

What are your thoughts?

What does this mean to me?
I know I am not the best baseball player on my team. I don't always hit the ball or catch it, but I know that by practicing I will get better. Be your own coach.

If you don't go after what you want, you'll never have it. If you don't ask, the answer is always no. If you don't step forward you are always in the same place.

– Nora Roberts

What are your thoughts?

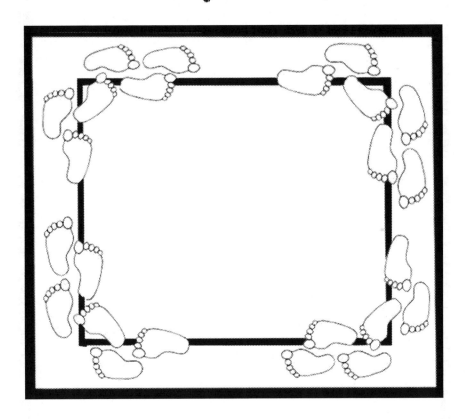

What does this mean to me?
I think of my daddy when we read this one. He works in sales and sometimes people tell him "no" instead of "yes." He keeps trying until he gets a "yes." Never quit.

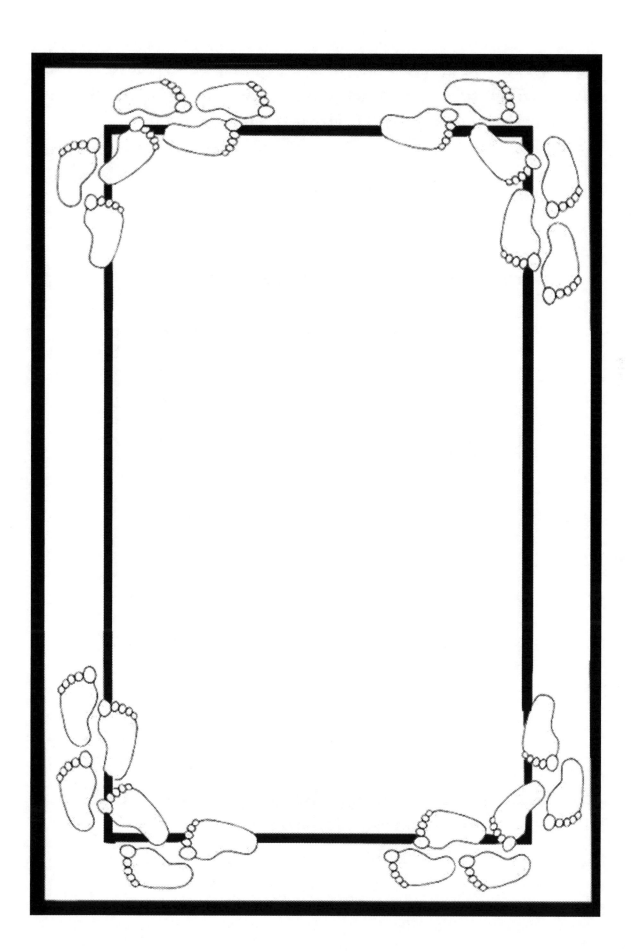

You will meet two kinds of people in life: ones who build you up and ones who tear you down. But in the end, you'll thank them both.

-Heidi Lamberton

What do you think?

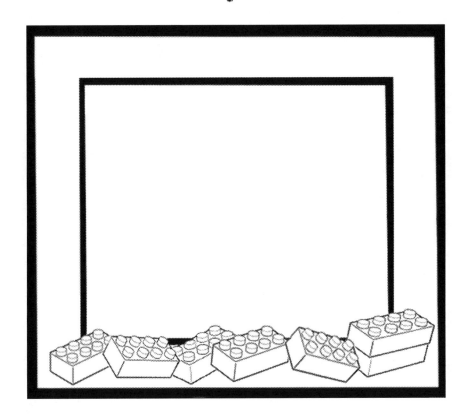

What does this mean to me?
I had a boy in my daycare and he would say very mean things to me and pick on me. I learned to not say mean things to other people and not pick on them. Learn from others.

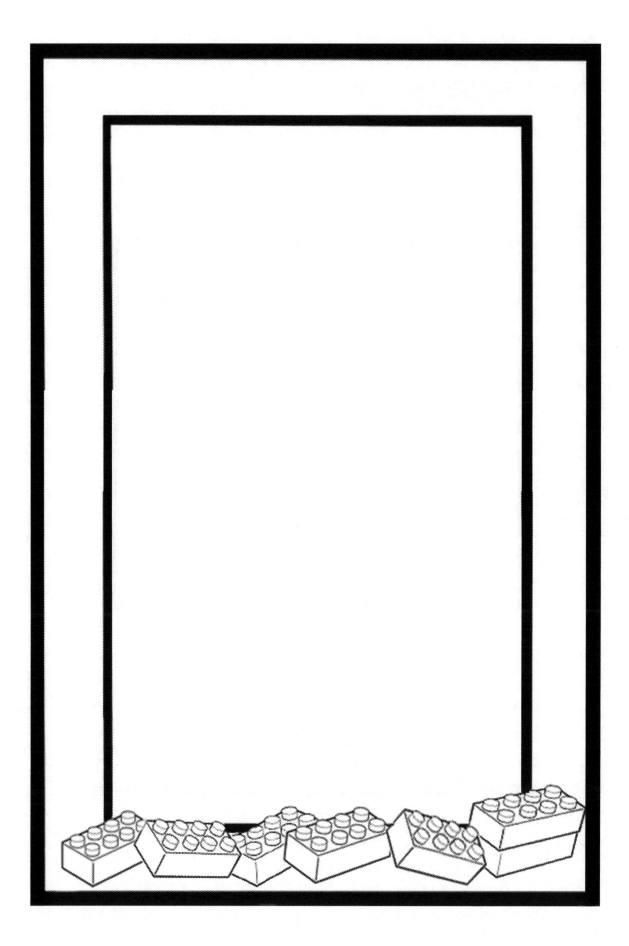

Love me when I least deserve it because that is when I really need it

-Swedish proverb

What do you think?

What does this mean to me?
Sometimes I don't want to pick up my toys in the basement. I get angry about it and am not nice to my parents. I know that I should pick them up and be nice. Even though I misbehave I still want my parents to love and hug me. Love people at their worst.

Be who you are and say what you feel because those who mind don't matter and those who matter don't mind.

-Dr. Seuss

What do you think?

What does this mean to me?
I try to tell my mom how I am feeling even when I feel mad and upset. She listens and tries to help. Be true to yourself. Express your feelings.

The best and most beautiful thing in the world cannot be seen or even touched, they must be felt with the heart.

-Helen Keller

What do you think?

What does this mean to me?
I have a favorite teacher at school, she always listens to me and gives me hugs. It makes me happy. Hearts gets happy from kindness.

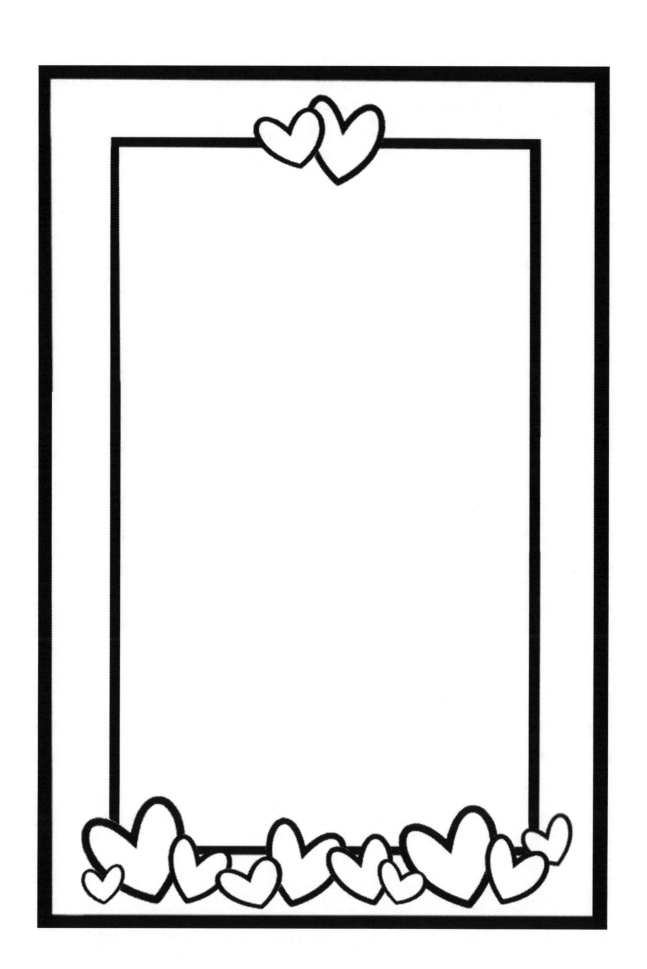

Sometimes, said Pooh, the smallest things take up the most room in you hear.
-A.A. Milne, Winnie-the-Pooh

What are your thoughts?

What does this mean to me?
I think about my little brother. He is one year old and small but I love him so much. Great people and things can be small.

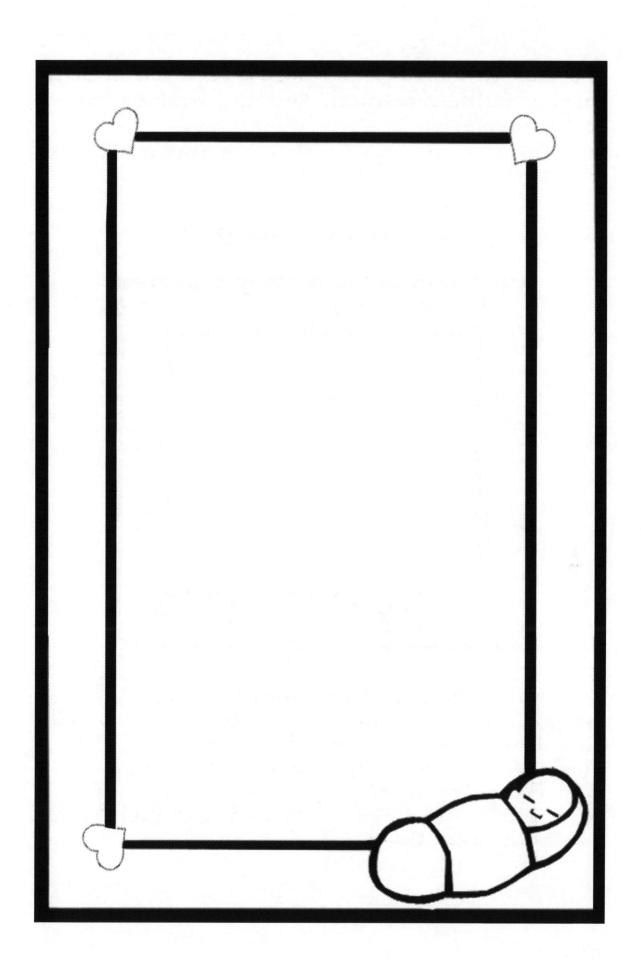

The first to apologize is the bravest. The first to forgive is the strongest. And the first to forget is the happiest.

– Imam Ali Casj

What are your thoughts?

What does this mean to me?
I fight sometimes with my brother Jake. I will take toys from him that he is playing with. I don't like to share sometimes with him. When I take things from him I know it is wrong and when I tell him I am sorry I always feel better. Apologies heal the heart.

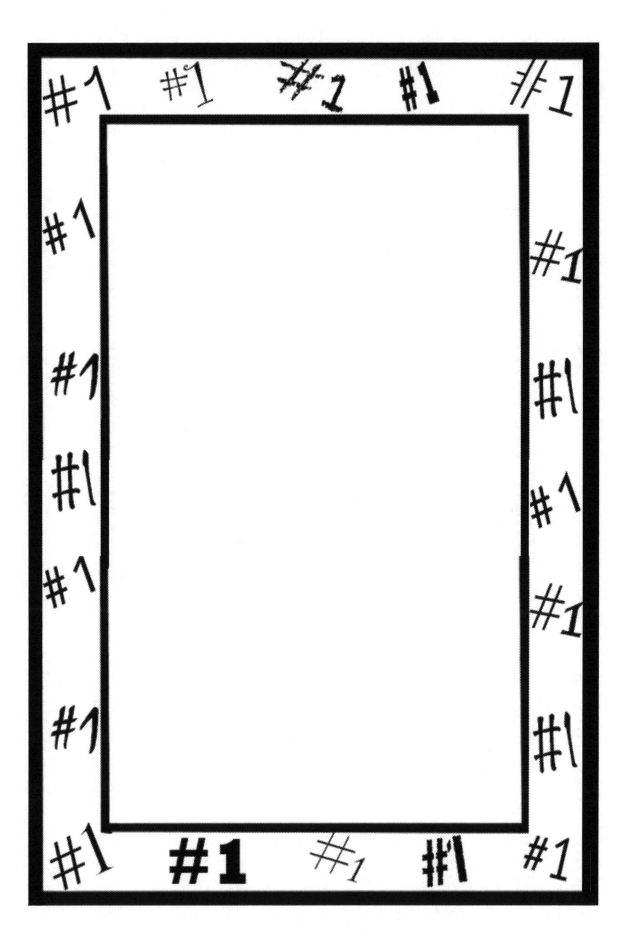

Love you to the moon and back.

                                         -Sam McBratney

What are your thoughts?

What does this mean to me?
We always say this in our family. We love each other a bunch, like more than a million times. Love is big.

We added in a couple pages to get you started.
Hugs. Andrew and Mommy

What are the quotes you want to add?